Congressional
Research
Service

The Article V Convention for Proposing Constitutional Amendments: Historical Perspectives for Congress

Thomas H. Neale
Specialist in American National Government

October 22, 2012

Congressional Research Service

7-5700

www.crs.gov

R42592

Summary

The Philadelphia Convention of 1787 provided two methods of proposing amendments to the U.S. Constitution. In the first, Congress, by two-thirds vote in both houses, proposes amendments to the states. If three-fourths of the states (38 at present) vote to ratify the amendment, it becomes part of the Constitution. Since 1789, Congress has proposed 33 amendments by this method, 27 of which have been adopted. In the second method, if the legislatures of two-thirds of the states (34 at present) apply, Congress must call a convention to consider and propose amendments, which must meet the same 38-state ratification requirement. This alternative, known as the Article V Convention, has not been implemented to date. Several times during the 20th century, organized groups promoted a convention that they hoped would propose amendments to the states, or to "prod" Congress to propose amendments they favored. The most successful was the movement for direct election of Senators, which helped prod Congress to propose the 17th Amendment. The most recent, which promoted a convention to consider a balanced federal budget amendment, gained 32 applications, just two short of the constitutional threshold. When the balanced budget amendment campaign failed in the 1980s, interest in the convention option faded and remained largely dormant for more than 20 years.

Within the past decade, interest in the Article V Convention process has reawakened: several policy advocacy organizations have publicized the Article V Convention option, particularly as an alternative to what they portray as a legislative and policy deadlock at the federal level. An important issue in the contemporary context is the fact that advances in communications technology could facilitate the emergence of technology-driven issue advocacy groups favorable to this phenomenon. The rise of instant interpersonal communications, email, and other social media helped facilitate the rapid growth of such groups as MoveOn.org, the Tea Party movement, and, most recently, Occupy Wall Street. These tools could be harnessed to promote a credible campaign in a much shorter time than was the case with previous convention advocacy movements.

Reviewing the history of the Article V Convention alternative, the record of the Constitutional Convention of 1787 clearly demonstrated the founders' original intent. During the convention, they agreed that a second mode of amendment was needed to balance the grant of amendatory power to Congress. This method, clearly identified in Article V as co-equal to congressional proposal of amendments, empowered the people, acting through their state legislatures, to summon a convention that would have equal authority to propose an amendment or amendments, which would then be presented to the states for ratification.

Only the states can summon an Article V Convention, by application from their legislatures. Some of the issues concerning this process include procedures within the state legislatures; the scope and conditions of applications for a convention; steps in submitting applications to Congress; and the role of the state governors in the process.

This report identifies and examines these issues; a companion report, CRS Report R42589, *The Article V Convention to Propose Constitutional Amendments: Contemporary Issues for Congress*, identifies contemporary issues for Congress and analyzes the congressional role in the Article V Convention process in greater detail.

Contents

Contacts

Introduction

Article V of the U.S. Constitution provides two methods of amendment for the nation's fundamental charter. In the first, Congress, by a two-thirds vote of both chambers, proposes amendments to the states, which then consider the proposal; if three-fourths (38 at present) approve the amendment, it is ratified, and becomes part of the Constitution. Beginning with the Bill of Rights in 1789, this method has been used to propose 33 amendments, 27 of which have been ratified.

Article V also offers an alternative method in which a convention to consider amendments is called by Congress on the application of the legislatures of two-thirds of the states (34 at present). The second constitutional amendment option, generally known as the "Article V Convention," has never been successfully used to propose an amendment to the Constitution. This report offers perspectives for Congress on the Article V Convention, opening with an overview of the provisions in Article V that established the convention procedure. The report further examines its origins at the Constitutional Convention of 1787; the history of the convention alternative, focusing on three major 20th century campaigns to convene a constitutional convention; and the role of the states in the Article V Convention process.

A companion report, CRS Report R42589, *The Article V Convention to Propose Constitutional Amendments: Contemporary Issues for Congress*, provides a comprehensive analysis of congressional issues, including information on the contemporary resurgence of interest in the convention alternative and the authority of Congress to call a convention; provide a framework and procedures for an Article V Convention; and submit proposed amendments to the states for ratification. It also identifies other elements in the process, including the President's role; the operation of checks and balances in the convention alternative; questions concerning a convention's composition and method of voting; and the function of the District of Columbia and U.S. territories.

Congress and the Article V Convention in the 21st Century

Congress is daily confronted with many competing demands for its time and energy; in light of these, what compelling interest should Congress have in the Article V Convention alternative in the 21st century?

First, Article V vests important and exclusive responsibilities over the amendment process in Congress. As noted previously, these include the right to propose amendments directly to the states for their consideration, and the responsibility to call a convention for proposing amendments on application of the legislatures of two-thirds of the states.

Second, while the Constitution is silent on the mechanics of an Article V Convention, Congress has historically laid claim to broad responsibilities in connection with a convention, including receiving, judging, and recording state applications; establishing procedures to summon a convention; setting the amount of time allotted to its deliberations, determining the number and selection process of its delegates; setting internal convention procedures, and providing arrangement for the formal transmission of any proposed amendments to the states. These issues are addressed in detail in the companion to this report, CRS Report R42589, *The Article V Convention to Propose Constitutional Amendments: Contemporary Issues for Congress.*

It may be argued that there is no pressing need for Congress to examine its Article V options and responsibilities. Historical precedent suggests that attaining petitions from two-thirds of the states necessary for an Article V Convention in a timely manner is a difficult obstacle, as demonstrated by several unsuccessful convention drives in the latter part of the 20th century. These fell short of the two-thirds mark, despite the vigorous efforts of organized support groups over a period of several years; moreover, until recently, there has been little apparent interest in the Article V Convention mechanism in the states since the 1980s. Judging by the historical record, the process might arguably be described as a footnote to constitutional history. The measured pace of the legislative process in the states has also traditionally served as an additional check to haste in calling such a convention.[1] For instance, in the case of the balanced budget amendment convention drive of the 1970s and 1980s, it took seven years for an organized campaign to gain convention applications from 32 states, two short of the two-thirds required in Article V.[2]

Although the Article V Convention device is not widely known or understood at present, it could provide a vehicle for issue organizations and coalitions seeking amendments to the Constitution. Given the extraordinary speed and flexibility of contemporary social media and communications technology, interested organizations could conceivably launch an Article V Convention campaign for a specific amendment or amendments, or perhaps for a general constitutional convention, within a shortened time frame. In the 1960s, 1970s, and 1980s, it took time for "grass roots" efforts to emerge, form organizations to promote their cause, communicate with like-minded groups, undertake campaigns in state legislatures, and generally to learn and perfect the ancillary skills necessary for nationwide issue advocacy. By comparison, the contemporary availability of instant interpersonal electronic communication, email, and other social network media can facilitate remarkably rapid growth in awareness of a political phenomenon. For instance, MoveOn.org emerged in 1998 as an ad hoc on-line coalition opposed to the impeachment of President Bill Clinton and grew quickly to a membership of 5 million.[3] More recently, the Tea Party movement originated in late 2008 with online discussions in conservative-oriented social networking sites and frequent conference calls among organizers. On February 19, 2009, a cable network business commentator made an on-air call for rallies to oppose government spending; his emotionally charged remarks were picked up by cable news networks and various websites, and

---

[1] As Supreme Court Justice and constitutional commentator Joseph Story noted, "The great principle to be sought is to make the changes practicable, but not too easy; to secure due deliberation, and caution; and to follow experience, rather than to open a way for experiments, suggested by mere speculation or theory." See Joseph Story, *Commentaries on the Constitution of the United States* (Boston: Hilliard, Gray & Co., 1833), §1821. Available in *The Founders Constitution*, a joint venture of the University of Chicago Press and the Liberty Fund, Web edition, at http://press-pubs.uchicago.edu/founders/documents/a5s12.html.

[2] See later in this report, under "The Balanced Budget Amendment: 1975-1983." While most state legislatures convene annually, their sessions are frequently limited by law; 32 states place some form of time constraint on their sessions, frequently limiting them to as little as 60 to 90 session days. Given the generally hectic pace and urgent demands faced by most state legislatures during their sessions, it seems unlikely that Article V Convention proposals could make it through the legislatures of 34 states in one year. Judging from previous efforts, it appears more likely that even a well-publicized and popular Article V petition drive would require two to five years of state legislative action before it approached "critical mass." See *The Book of the States*, 2009 edition, volume 41 (Lexington, KY: Council of State Governments, 2009), pp. 83-85.

[3] Jonathan Rauch, "How Tea Party Organizes Without Leaders," *National Journal*, September 11, 2010, available at http://www.nationaljournal.com/njmagazine/cs_20100911_8855.php .

---

went "viral." In just two months the newly named "Tea Party" movement was able to convene over 600,000 supporters in more than 600 demonstrations around the nation.[4]

In a related development, over the past few years, interest has grown in several new constitutional amendment proposals, such as the "Repeal Amendment," which would provide for the repeal of any federal legislation by a vote of disapproval in the legislatures of two-thirds of the states.[5] Another recent proposal would repeal the 17th Amendment, and restore the election of U.S. Senators to state legislatures.[6] Given the advances in communications technology cited above, groups supporting these measures or others might find the Article V Convention to be an attractive vehicle for the promotion of their proposed amendments. Under these circumstances, Congress might be called on to revisit the Article V Convention issue for the first time since the 1980s.

The obstacles, however, remain daunting, even in the face of rapid change: the Constitution sets a considerable hurdle for the Article V Convention process by requiring that applications for a convention be made by the legislatures of at least two-thirds of the several states. Further, any amendments proposed would face the same task of securing approval of three-fourths of the states before they were ratified.

Constitutional Provisions: Article V Offers Two Modes of Amendment

Article V of the U.S. Constitution provides two methods for amending the nation's fundamental charter. The first method, and to date the only one used successfully, authorizes proposal of amendments by Congress:

> The Congress, whenever two thirds of both Houses shall deem it necessary, shall propose Amendments to this Constitution, ... which ... shall be valid to all Intents and Purposes, as Part of this Constitution, when ratified by the Legislatures of three fourths of the several States, or by Conventions in three fourths thereof, as the one or the other Mode of Ratification may be proposed by the Congress; ....[7]

As noted in Article V, amendments ratified by the states under either procedure are indistinguishable and have equal force; they are both "valid to all Intents and Purposes, as Part of this Constitution ...."[8]

---

[4] Ibid.

[5] Kate Zernicke, "Proposed Amendment Would Enable States to Repeal Federal Law," *New York Times*, December 19, 2010, available at http://www.nytimes.com/2010/12/20/us/politics/20states.html.

[6] The Campaign to Restore Federalism, "Repeal the Seventeenth Amendment," available at http://www.restorefederalism.org/?gclid=CK386ay3pa4CFSEQNAodaTKFRw.

[7] U.S. Constitution, Article V.

[8] Ibid.

Proposal of Amendments by Congress

Congress has used this first, or "congressional," amendment process to propose 33 amendments to the states since 1789, 27 of which have been successfully ratified to date.

Constitutional Provisions

Key constitutional elements include the following:

- Amendments proposed by Congress must be approved by two-thirds vote in both the House of Representatives and the Senate.

- The proposed amendment must be subsequently ratified by three-fourths of the legislatures of the states, 38 at present.

- Alternatively, Congress may direct that ratifications shall be by ad hoc conventions called by the states for the specific purpose of considering the ratification.[9]

- The same three-fourths requirement for adoption would also apply if Congress voted to require ratification by ad hoc state conventions.

Supplementary Provisions

Over the years, Congress has added four additional elements in the amendment process that were not included in the text of Article V.

- First, the congressional vote to propose an amendment must be approved by a *two-thirds vote of the Members present and voting, a quorum being present*, in both the House and Senate. The Supreme Court ruled in *National Prohibition Cases* of 1920 that Congress had the authority to set these thresholds.[10]

- Second, amendments are not incorporated into the existing text of the Constitution as adopted in 1788, but rather, are included as supplementary articles.[11]

- Third, beginning in the 20th century, Congress has required that ratifications must be roughly contemporaneous, and has set a seven-year deadline for the 18th and 20th Amendments[12] and all subsequent proposed amendments.[13] This practice was

---

[9] To date, Congress has specified ratification by ad hoc state convention for only one amendment, the 21st, which repealed the 18th (Prohibition) Amendment.

[10] This was one of two questions decided by the Supreme Court in the *National Prohibition Cases* (253 U.S. 350 (1920)).

[11] James Madison, sponsor in the House of Representatives of the amendments now known as the Bill of Rights, suggested they should be incorporated in the body of the Constitution. The House decided instead to add them to the end of the Constitution as additional articles, a precedent followed for all subsequent amendments.

[12] After setting a deadline for the 18th Amendment, Congress did not include a ratification deadline for the 19th, but resumed the practice with the 20th through 26th Amendments (and the proposed Equal Rights and District of Columbia Congressional Representation Amendments, which were not ratified). The seven-year requirement was incorporated in the body of the amendment in the 18th and 20th through 22nd Amendments. For subsequent amendments, Congress concluded that incorporating the time limit in the amendment itself "cluttered up" the amendment. Consequently, the (continued...)

upheld by the Supreme Court in its 1921 ruling, *Dillon v. Gloss*,[14] later confirmed in 1939 in *Coleman v. Miller*.[15]

- Finally, the Constitution does not require approval of proposed amendments by Presidents, who have no function in the process of proposing an amendment to the states. Their approval or signature has no bearing on the process, and they cannot veto or pocket veto proposed amendments that have been approved by the requisite congressional majorities or by an Article V Convention.[16]

Proposal of Amendments by an Article V Convention

The second method provided in Article V empowers the states to petition Congress for a convention to consider amendments. This procedure is generally known as the Article V Convention.

Constitutional Provisions

Key constitutional elements include the following:

- The legislatures of two-thirds of the states, 34 at present, must present applications to Congress.

- Congress shall then "call a Convention for proposing Amendments."

- Amendments proposed by an Article V Convention must also be ratified by three-fourths of the states.

- Congress may provide for consideration of such amendment either by state legislatures or ad hoc state ratification conventions, at its discretion.

(...continued)

23rd through 26th Amendments placed the limit in the authorizing resolution, rather than in the body of the amendment. See "Article V: Ratification" in U.S. Congress, Senate, *The Constitution of the United States, Analysis and Interpretation*, 108th Congress, Senate Document 108-17 (Washington: GPO, 2004), available at http://www.gpoaccess.gov/constitution/pdf2002/015.pdf.

[13] The 27th Amendment, the most recently ratified, was proposed to the states in 1789 *without* a seven-year time limit on ratification. After 203 years, as a "pending" amendment, it was revived, ratified by more states, and was recognized as part of the Constitution in 1992. Congress extended the deadline for ratification of the proposed Equal Rights Amendment by 39 months, from March, 1979 to June, 1982, but the Amendment still failed to garner the 38 necessary state ratifications before the extended deadline.

[14] *Dillon v. Gloss*, 256 U.S. 368 (1921).

[15] *Coleman v. Miller*, 307 U.S. 443 (1939). The seven-year requirement was incorporated in the body of the amendment in the 18th and 20th through 22nd Amendments. For subsequent amendments, Congress concluded that incorporating the time limit in the amendment itself "cluttered up" the amendment. Consequently, the 23rd through 26th Amendments placed the limit in the authorizing resolution, rather than in the body of the amendment. (See "Article V: Ratification" in U.S. Congress, Senate, *The Constitution of the United States, Analysis and Interpretation*, 108th Congress, Senate Document 108-17 (Washington: GPO, 2004), available at http://www.gpoaccess.gov/constitution/pdf2002/015.pdf.

[16] This issue was determined as part of a 1798 Supreme Court decision, *Hollingsworth v. Virginia*, 3 Dall. (3 U.S.) 378 (1798). The role of the President in the Article V Convention process is examined in greater detail in the companion to this report, CRS Report R42589, *The Article V Convention to Propose Constitutional Amendments: Contemporary Issues for Congress*, by Thomas H. Neale.

Supplementary Provisions

Of the supplementary requirements noted previously that have come to be associated with proposed amendments, at least three would arguably apply to those proposed by an Article V Convention. First, it is likely, but not certain, that an Article V Convention would follow the traditional practice of proposing amendments as addenda to the Constitution. Second, it is likely, but again not certain, that a seven-year time limit for ratification would be included in any proposed amendment or amendments. Finally, the President would also have no function in the proposal of amendments by a convention, as is the case with amendments proposed by Congress.

"Original Intent:" The Founders Include the Article V Convention Process in the U.S. Constitution

The idea that constitutional amendments might be drafted and forwarded directly to the states appeared early in the Constitutional Convention of 1787, when the "Virginia Plan" proposed amendment of the national charter, "whensoever it shall seem necessary, and that the assent of the National Legislature ought not to be required thereto."[17] During the course of convention proceedings, the amendment clause evolved; initially the states were to have sole authority to call a convention; Congress was then similarly empowered.[18] The debate reveals that the delegates were concerned that the amending process should not be lodged exclusively with Congress, but that the states should also have the opportunity to propose amendments, either directly, or via convention, although Alexander Hamilton asserted that the national legislature (Congress) "will be the first to perceive and will be the most sensible to the necessity of amendments...."[19] On September 10, Article V began to assume its final form when James Madison offered the following version, which rearranged the various elements that had been debated up to that point:

> The Legislature of the U.S. whenever two thirds of both Houses shall deem necessary, or on the application of two thirds of the Legislatures of the several States, shall propose amendments to this Constitution, which shall be valid to all intents and purposes as part thereof, when the same shall have been ratified by three fourths at least of the Legislatures of the several States, or by Conventions in three fourths thereof, as one or the other mode of ratification may be proposed by the Legislature of the U.S. ....[20]

Two amendments to the article were added in the convention's final sessions. The first, which prohibited any interference with the slave trade before 1808, was included at the insistence of the slave-holding states, while the second, which guaranteed that no state could be deprived of equal suffrage in the Senate without its consent, was inserted to reassure the less populous states that the formula providing for equal state representation in the Senate would not be altered at some

---

[17] U.S. Constitutional Convention, *The Debates in the Federal Convention of 1787 Which Framed the Constitution of the United States of America, reported by James Madison* (Greenwood Press, Westport, CT: 1970, c. 1920, Oxford University Press), p. 29, hereinafter referred to as *Madison's Notes*.

[18] For an account of convention debate arranged by article, rather than by session, consult *The Founders' Constitution*, Web edition, available at http://press-pubs.uchicago.edu/founders/.

[19] *Madison's Notes*, p. 539.

[20] Ibid., p. 540.

---

future time: "[t]his motion being dictated by the circulating murmurs of the small States was agreed to without debate, no one opposing it, or on the question, saying no."[21]

The Federalist confirms the convention's intent that the process of proposing amendments should be entrusted to both Congress *and* the state legislatures. As James Madison wrote in *Federalist 43*, "Powers Delegated to the General Government: III,"

> The mode [of amendment] preferred by the Convention seems to be stamped with every mark of propriety. It guards equally against that extreme facility which would render the Constitution too mutable; and that extreme difficulty which might perpetuate its discovered faults. *It moreover equally enables the general and the state governments to originate the amendment of errors as they may be pointed out by the experience on one side or on the other* (emphasis added).[22]

Alexander Hamilton commented more specifically on the state petition process as a potential remedy to congressional inaction in *Federalist 85*, "Conclusion:"

> In opposition to the probability of subsequent amendments, it has been urged that the persons delegated to the administration of the national government will always be disinclined to yield up any portion of the authority of which they were once possessed..... The intrinsic difficulty of governing thirteen states ... will, in my opinion, constantly impose on the national rulers the necessity of a spirit of accommodation to the reasonable expectations of their constituents. But there is yet a further consideration.... [i]t is this, that the national rulers, whenever nine States concur, will have no option on the subject. By the fifth article of the plan, the Congress will be obliged ... to call a convention for proposing amendments.... The words of this article are peremptory. The Congress "shall call a convention." Nothing in this particular is left to the discretion of that body.[23]

Constitutional scholar and commentator St. George Tucker, a friend and contemporary of the Virginia delegates to the Philadelphia Convention, noted that

> ... the fifth article of the Constitution provides the mode by which future amendments to the [C]onstitution may be proposed, discussed, and carried into effect.... And this be effected in two different modes: the first on recommendation from [C]ongress, whenever two thirds of both houses shall concur in the expediency of any amendment. The second, which secures to the states an influence in case [C]ongress should neglect to recommend such amendments, provides, that [C]ongress shall, on application from the legislatures of two thirds of the states, call a convention for proposing amendments.... Both of these provisions appear excellent. Of the utility and practicability of the former, we have already had most satisfactory experience. The latter will probably never be resorted to, unless the federal government should betray symptoms of corruption, which may render it expedient for the states to exert themselves in order to the application of some radical and effectual remedy.[24]

---

[21] Ibid., pp. 540, 575.

[22] James Madison, "Powers Delegated to the General Government: III," in *The Federalist*, Number 43(Cambridge, MA: The Belknap Press of Harvard University Press, 1961), p. 315.

[23] Alexander Hamilton, "Conclusion," in *The Federalist*, Number 85, Ibid., p. 546.

[24] St. George Tucker, *Blackstone's Commentaries: With Notes of Reference to the Constitution and Laws of the Federal Government of the United States and the Commonwealth of Virginia*, quoted in *The Founders' Constitution*, Web edition, available at http://press-pubs.uchicago.edu/founders/documents/a5s11.html.

On balance, the historical record indicates that the founders established the Article V state application process as a complement to the congressional process proposal, to ensure that a convention could be called even if Congress refused to consider an amendment or amendments, so long as the proposal enjoyed the supermajority support of two-thirds of the states.

Reviewing the convention record, one contemporary observer suggests that, notwithstanding the fact that all 27 current amendments were proposed by Congress, the founders had no intention that this should be the predominant or even preferred method of amending the Constitution:

> There is nothing to suggest that the Framers intended the congressional procedure to be the predominant amendment process. To the contrary, they felt that they had struck a proper balance in distributing the power to propose amendments, intending to express a preference for neither method.[25]

To sum up the available record indicating the founders' original intent, it appears that they crafted Article V very much in the spirit of checks and balances, and separation of powers, that permeates the Constitution. During the convention, they agreed that a second mode of amendment was needed to balance the grant of amendatory power to Congress. This method, clearly identified in Article V as co-equal to congressional proposal, empowers the people, acting through their state legislatures, to summon a convention that would have equal authority to propose an amendment or amendments, which are then proposed to the states for ratification. In *Federalist* 51, James Madison famously wrote, "If men were angels, no government would be necessary.... In framing a government which is to be to be administered by men over men the great difficulty is this: you must first enable the government to control the governed; and in the next place oblige it to control itself."[26] It appears that this principle was not far from their minds as they drafted Article V, because the convention provided an additional check on both methods of proposing amendments by requiring that all proposed amendments be approved by the legislatures of, or ad hoc conventions in, three-fourths of the several states, and further empowered Congress to select which mode of ratification it preferred.

Efforts to Summon an Article V Convention: The Experience of the 20th Century

Proposals for an Article V Convention are as old as the republic. The first of more than 700 was filed in 1789, the same year government under the U.S. Constitution was established, but over the next century, only 23 applications were received by Congress.[27] In fact, the Article V Convention

---

[25] Michael A. Almond, "Amendment by Convention: Our Next Constitutional Crisis?" *North Carolina Law Review*, vol. 53, issue 3, February 1975, p. 498.

[26] James Madison, in *The Federalist*, Number 51, "Checks and Balances," p. 356.

[27] Statistics provided by Friends of the Article V Convention (FOAVC), and are available at http://foa5c.org/file.php/1/ Articles/AmendmentsTables.htm. It should be noted that these figures are not official, but were compiled by FOAVC. The base compilation, taken from *Annals of Congress*, *Congressional Debates*, *Congressional Globe*, and *Congressional Record*, appeared in "A Lawful and Peaceful Revolution: Article V and Congress' Present Duty to Call a Convention for Considering Amendments," an article that appeared in *Hamline Law Review*, volume 14, number 1, fall 1990, pp. 1-116. Subsequent updates were compiled by FOAVC; this organization's list is evidently the only comprehensive compilation of state applications. Neither Congress, which receives state applications for an Article V Convention, nor the National Archives, which is the custodian of most congressional documents, retains the applications in an organized collection. Congressional procedures concerning the disposition state applications are (continued...)

is sometimes referred to as a 20th century phenomenon, because 697 of the 743 applications recorded by the Friends of the Article V Convention were filed between 1900 and 1999.[28] These have included applications for a general convention, as well as petitions for a convention to consider a particular amendment in an estimated 47 issue areas.[29] Perhaps the first example of what could be considered a "campaign" to promote state applications actually began late in the 19th century with the movement in favor of an amendment providing direct election of U.S. Senators. The following section examines this movement and two others, one favoring an amendment concerning apportionment in the state legislatures, and a third advocating a convention to propose an amendment requiring a balanced federal budget. These "case studies" provide a more detailed look at one campaign that accomplished its ultimate goal, direct election of Senators, albeit without an Article V Convention, and two that came very close to meeting the constitutional threshold of applications from two-thirds of the states.

Direct Election of Senators, 1893-1912

The campaign for direct election of Senators arguably provides the first example of an organized campaign for an Article V Convention. Activity in support of direct election did not approach the sophistication of a modern advocacy campaign, that is, one possessing a national organizational structure and local affiliates, with a defined mission statement or manifesto, that raises funds from private donors and conducts a sustained and coordinated advocacy campaign on various levels and media. It did, however, embrace like-minded groups and individuals working cooperatively toward a common goal.

During the last third of the 19th century, the U.S. Senate was troubled by a growing number of sometimes lengthy vacancies, as politically deadlocked state legislatures proved unable to agree on candidates for the office.[30] In addition, Senators were seen as increasingly influenced, and in some cases their elections were influenced by, corporate and monopoly interests.[31] Public opinion, and pro-reform groups, particularly in the Progressive and Populist movements, looked to direct popular election as a remedy for these conditions. The House of Representatives proposed a relevant amendment as early as 1894, but direct election amendments in the Senate never reached the floor during this period.[32]

While states had previously petitioned Congress to propose an amendment providing direct election, in 1893 Nebraska's legislature went a step further to revive the long-neglected provision of Article V that empowers states to apply to Congress for a convention to consider amendments

---

(...continued)

examined in greater detail in the companion to this report, CRS Report for Congress CRS Report R42589, *The Article V Convention to Propose Constitutional Amendments: Contemporary Issues for Congress*, by Thomas H. Neale, under the heading "Receiving and Processing the State Applications: Existing Procedures and Potential Revision."

[28] FOAVC website, available at http://foa5c.org/file.php/1/Articles/AmendmentsTables.htm#Table01.

[29] Ibid.

[30] Recall that Article I, Section 3, clause 1 of the Constitution originally provided that Senators would be "chosen by the Legislature" in each state.

[31] David Graham Philips's series, "The Treason of the Senate," published in 1906 in *Cosmopolitan* epitomized the case for reform. See, for instance, "The Treason of the Senate: Aldrich, the Head of It All," *Cosmopolitan*, March 1906, available at http://www.wwnorton.com/college/history/archive/resources/documents/ch24_02.htm.

[32] Alan P. Grimes, *Democracy and the Amendments to the Constitution*, (Lexington, MA: Lexington Books, D.C. Heath and Co., 1978), pp. 75-78.

---

to the Constitution. In a classic example of a state acting as a "laboratory of democracy," the Pennsylvania legislature in 1899 approved a "model" application for an Article V Convention, which it then circulated among secretaries of state (or the equivalent officer) in all the other states.[33] The wording of Pennsylvania's application reflected growing support for a convention: whereas earlier state applications had requested Congress to propose a direct election amendment, the language of the model application instead *directed* Congress to summon a convention, reflecting Article V's admonition that Congress "*shall call* a Convention for proposing Amendments (emphasis added)...."[34] Over the next decade, more than 25 states took similar action and applied for a convention, while others found a way around the constitutional provision empowering state legislatures to choose U.S. Senators. During this period, many states adopted some version of the "Oregon Plan," by which state legislators committed themselves during their own election campaigns to vote for the Senate candidate who won the most popular votes in an all-party "advisory" primary. As the number of "Oregon Plan" Senators grew, attitudes in the upper house began to change, and in 1912, the Senate joined the House in proposing what became the 17th Amendment to the Constitution.[35]

The concerted action of states in calling for an Article V Convention with the ultimate purpose of convincing Congress to propose a particular amendment has been referred to as the "prodding effect," because the states are *prodding* Congress to take the initiative. The events leading to proposal of the 17th Amendment arguably comprise the most successful example of the prodding effect to date.[36]

As the 20th century progressed, the Article V Convention device enjoyed mixed success on the state level. State legislatures filed applications for a convention to consider amendments in a range of public policy issues, including repeal of the 16th (income tax) and 18th (prohibition) Amendments, limitation on federal taxes, and prohibition of busing to achieve racial balance in schools, among others. None of these, however, approached the requisite number necessary for a convention. The most successful drives for an Article V Convention, which approached the 34-state constitutional threshold, came in the second half of the century and concerned two politically sensitive issues: apportionment in state legislatures and an amendment requiring a balanced federal budget.

State Legislative Apportionment, 1964-1969

The first instance of a substantial campaign for an Article V Convention following the successful proposal of the 17th Amendment occurred in the 1960s in response to a Supreme Court ruling on apportionment of state legislatures. In 1964, the High Court ruled in *Reynolds v. Sims*[37] that

---

[33] Russell L. Caplan, *Constitutional Brinkmanship, Amending the Constitution by National Convention* (New York: Oxford University Press, 1988), p. 63.

[34] Ibid.

[35] For a history of the 17th Amendment, see George H. Haynes, *The Senate of the United States, Its History and Practice* (Boston: Houghton Mifflin, 1938), volume 1, pp. 79-117; and Grimes, *Democracy and the Amendments to the Constitution*, pp. 74-82.

[36] For further information on the prodding effect, see Charles W. Hucker, "Constitutional Convention Poses Questions," *Congressional Quarterly Weekly Report*, volume 37, February 17, 1979, pp. 273-276; or James Kenneth Rogers, "The Other Way to Amend the Constitution: The Article V Constitutional Convention Amendment Process," *Harvard Journal of Law and Public Policy*, volume 30, number 3, 2007, pp. 1008-1010.

[37] *Reynolds v. Sims*, 377 U.S. 533 (1964).

districts in both chambers of state legislatures must be generally equal in population, thus embracing the principle, "one person, one vote."[38] Up to that time, states had routinely created legislative districts of different populations; most notably, less populous districts were drawn in rural areas as a means of preserving a degree of influence for "farm interests" and "the rural vote." Critics of the Supreme Court's ruling expressed fear that it would lead to excessive dominance of state governments by "urban interests."[39] Conservatives also countered the Court's decision with the states-rights centered argument that it encouraged what they characterized as a federal encroachment on state authority.[40]

Congressional foes of both *Reynolds v. Sims* and subsequent related Supreme Court decisions were headed by Everett M. Dirksen of Illinois, Republican leader in the Senate. Opponents first attempted to delay implementation of the Supreme Court's decision through legislation; failing in that, Senator Dirksen then introduced S.J.Res. 2 in the 89th Congress, a constitutional amendment that would have permitted states to use additional factors besides population in apportioning one chamber of their legislatures. He was able to attach this resolution as an amendment in the nature of a substitute to a non-controversial measure, S.J.Res. 66, designating National American Legion Baseball Week, but the amended proposal failed to win the necessary two-thirds margin in the Senate.[41]

While supporters of the Dirksen proposal continued to introduce amendments in Congress, and Senator Dirksen himself continued to promote a one-house exemption from *Reynolds v. Sims*, the focus switched to an Article V Convention. In late 1964, the General Assembly of the Council of State Governments endorsed the one-house state apportionment exception, and published and circulated both a manual on the Article V Convention process for state legislatures and a model application for a convention.[42] The first state applications for a convention to consider amendments on legislative apportionment were submitted in 1963, and by the 91st Congress (1969-1970), 33 states had filed Article V applications, just one short of the two-thirds necessary to trigger a convention. The 33rd petition proved to be the high-water mark for the legislative apportionment campaign, however. As the prospect of an Article V Convention became more and more likely, opposition increased, much of which was generated by warnings about the dangers of a runaway convention,[43] and several state legislatures reconsidered their actions. According to one commentator, "[i]n some of the state legislatures approving applications, the members thought they were merely expressing disagreement with the Supreme Court decisions and did not appreciate the legal implications of their vote."[44] Four states subsequently rescinded their

---

[38] *Reynolds v. Sims* was one of three Supreme Court decisions relating to apportionment matters delivered in the first half of the 1960s. In *Baker v. Carr*, (389 U.S. 186 (1962)), the Court ruled that apportionment was a justiciable question, whereas previously it had been considered political and not subject to court action. In *Wesberry v. Sanders* (376 U.S. 1 (1964)), it ruled that U.S. House of Representatives districts must have substantially equal populations.

[39] Caplan, *Constitutional Brinksmanship*, p. 73.

[40] James Stasny, "The Constitutional Convention Provision of Article V: Historical Perspectives," *Cooley Law Review*, volume 1, issue 1, 1982-83, p. 85.

[41] "33 States Call for Constitutional Convention to Revise One-Man-One-Vote Ruling," *Congressional Quarterly's Guide to the Congress of the United States* (Congressional Quarterly Service: Washington, 1971), pp. 288-289.

[42] Stasny, "The Constitutional Convention Provision of Article V: Historical Perspectives," p. 88.

[43] A runaway Article V Convention is generally defined as one that was summoned to consider a particular issue, e.g., legislative apportionment in the states, but which also investigated other constitutional issues. The runaway convention phenomenon is examined in greater length in the companion to this report, CRS Report R42589, *The Article V Convention to Propose Constitutional Amendments: Contemporary Issues for Congress*, by Thomas H. Neale.

[44] Caplan, *Constitutional Brinksmanship*, p. 74.

---

applications, while the unexpected death of Senator Dirksen in September 1969 deprived the movement of its strongest public advocate and marked the effective end of the campaign.[45]

The Balanced Budget Amendment, 1975-1983

Although amendments to control federal spending or cap federal budget deficits were introduced in Congress as early as the 1930s, the first organized movement to call an Article V Convention to consider a balanced budget amendment got under way in the mid-1970s.

According to several accounts,[46] the impetus was provided by the National Taxpayers Union (NTU), which describes itself in its contemporary literature as "a nonprofit, non-partisan citizen group whose members work every day for lower taxes and smaller government at all levels."[47] NTU used its staff and resources to promote the concept of an Article V balanced budget convention, preparing model legislation and establishing informal networks of supportive state legislators.[48] Throughout the decade of the 1970s, a widespread wave of public interest in restraining tax increases provided a favorable environment for the movement. In California and Massachusetts, ballot initiatives setting limits to state and local tax levels and increases were approved; California Governor Edmund G. "Jerry" Brown endorsed the idea in his 1979 inaugural address;[49] and Senator Robert Dole recommended it for its potential value in "prodding" Congress to give serious consideration to a congressionally proposed amendment.[50] Four states joined the drive in 1975, followed by eight in 1976, five in 1977, five in 1978, and eight more in May 1979, for a total of 30 applications, four fewer than the constitutional threshold.[51] Most of the state applications calling for a balanced budget convention during this period were conditional, calling on Congress to propose an amendment, and stating that if Congress failed to do so, then the resolution should be considered a state application for an Article V Convention.[52]

As the number of state applications mounted, critics mobilized to oppose the campaign; a counter-convention group, Citizens for the Constitution, was established to make the case against an Article V balanced budget amendment convention. The newly formed organization described that effort as a stealth campaign: Vice President Walter Mondale's chief of staff asserted that, "[t]hey were remarkably successful until it became known what they were doing.... Nobody was paying any attention."[53] Some opponents claimed that a balanced budget amendment would place federal finances in a "straight jacket," while others warned against the dangers of a runaway convention. Supporters of the convention accused the opposition of using "scare tactics," but the campaign appeared to lose momentum. New applications "no longer breezed thorough state

---

[45] Ibid., p. 76.

[46] Gerald Gunther, "The Convention Method of Amending the United States Constitution," *Georgia Law Review*, volume 14, number 1, fall 1979, p.3; Charles Mohr, "Tax Union Playing Chief Role in Drive," *New York Times*, May 15, 1979, p D18.

[47] "About NTU," National Taxpayers Union website, available at http://www.ntu.org/about-ntu/.

[48] Caplan, *Constitutional Brinksmanship*, p. 79.

[49] Maryanne Rackoff, "The Monster Approaching the Capital: the Effort to Write Economic Policy into the Constitution," *Akron Law Review*, volume 15, issue 4, spring 1982, p. 733.

[50] Caplan, *Constitutional Brinksmanship*, p. 80.

[51] Mohr, "Tax Union Playing Chief Role in Drive," p. D18.

[52] Gunther, "The Convention System of Amending the United States Constitution," p. 3.

[53] Ibid.

legislative chambers, but on the contrary, faced tough, extended debate as lawmakers realized their votes mattered."[54]

The change in climate was reflected in state actions; no applications were filed with Congress in 1980 or 1981, and those of Alaska in 1982 and Missouri in 1983 proved to be the campaign's high water mark—no further applications were made for a convention to consider a balanced budget amendment.[55] Notwithstanding its failure to meet the constitutional hurdle, the campaign arguably contributed to a congressional response: acting in the context of the Article V Convention campaign, the 97th Congress (1981-1982) gave serious consideration to relevant proposals, culminating in the Senate's passage of a balanced budget amendment, S.J.Res. 58, by a bipartisan vote of 69-31 on August 4, 1982. A majority of Representatives favored the House version of the amendment, H.J.Res. 350, when it came to the floor on October 1, 1982, but the vote of 236 to 187 failed to meet the constitutional requirement of passage by two-thirds of Members present and voting.[56] Although partisans of the Article V Convention, supported by President Ronald Reagan, continued to press for additional support from the states, the 33rd and 34th applications remained elusive, and supporters increasingly turned to legislative alternatives.

In 1985, the 99th Congress passed the 1985 Gramm-Rudman-Hollings Balanced Budget and Emergency Deficit Control Act (GRH),[57] claiming that this legislation would serve the same purpose as an Article V Convention with less risk.[58] Concerns about a runaway convention and hopes that the 1985 passage of the Gramm-Rudman-Hollings Act would lead to a balanced federal budget have been credited with forestalling additional state applications for a convention.[59] Some years later, a balanced budget amendment proposal was included in the House Republicans' "Contract with America" policy manifesto in the 1994 congressional elections campaign. This measure, introduced as H.J.Res. 1 in the 104th Congress, passed in the House of Representatives by a vote of 300-132 on January 26, 1995;[60] On March 2, 1995, however, the Senate voted 65 to 35 in favor of the resolution, a margin that fell two votes short of the constitutionally mandated requirement that two-thirds of Members present and voting approve a proposed amendment.[61]

---

[54] Caplan, *Constitutional Brinksmanship*, p. 81.

[55] Congressional Research Service White Paper, *State Applications for a Constitutional Convention to Propose a Balanced Budget Amendment: Analysis and Legislative History*, by David C. Huckabee, (Washington: CRS, 1984) pp. 26-27. Available to Members of Congress and congressional staff from CRS.

[56] "Balanced Budget Drive Stalls in Congress," *Congress and the Nation*, volume VI, 1981-1984 (Washington: Congressional Quarterly, Inc., 1985), p. 52.

[57] Gramm-Rudman-Hollings Balanced Budget and Emergency Deficit Control Act of 1985, P.L. 99-177, 99 Stat 1038. Parts of the act were later declared unconstitutional by the Supreme Court in *Bowsher v. Synar*, 48 U.S. 714, (1986), and reenacted in different form as Title XIII in the Budget Enforcement Act of 1990, P.L. 101-508, 104 Stat. 1388. The Gramm-Rudman-Hollings Act was not notably successful in reducing federal budget deficits, but the Budget Enforcement Act and the buoyant national economy of the 1990s ultimately helped to reduce deficits, and produced surpluses in FY1998-FY2001. See U.S. Office of Management and Budget, *Budget of the United States Government, Fiscal Year 2009, Historical Tables*, Table 1-3, "Summary of Receipts, Outlays, Surpluses and Deficits ... 1940-2013," available at http://frwebgate3.access.gpo.gov/cgi-bin/TEXTgate.cgi?WAISdocID=qWxISN/23/1/0&WAISaction= retrieve.

[58] Caplan, *Constitutional Brinksmanship*, pp. 83-85.

[59] James Rogers, "The Other Way to Amend the Constitution: The Article V Constitutional Amendment Process," *Harvard Journal of Law and Public Policy*, vol. 30, number 3, summer, 2007, p. 1010.

[60] See House roll call 51, 104th Congress, first session, available at http://clerk.house.gov/evs/1995/roll051.xml.

[61] See Senate roll call vote number 98, 104th Congress, first session, available at http://www.senate.gov/legislative/LIS/ roll_call_lists/roll_call_vote_cfm.cfm?congress=104&session=1&vote=00098.

Although amendments to propose a balanced federal budget continue to be introduced in every Congress—25 in the 112th Congress by June 11, 2012—the campaign for an Article V Convention to propose such a measure had effectively ended by the mid-1980s. Eventually, a number of states reconsidered their applications for a convention: between 1988 and 2010, 17 state legislatures passed resolutions of rescission. In some cases, these resolutions rescinded *all* previous Article V applications, while others specifically cited a convention for a balanced budget amendment.[62]

Anticipating an Article V Convention: Legislative Proposals in the 93rd Through 102nd Congresses

Congress has addressed the convention issue with study and legislative proposals in the past, particularly in the 1970s and 1980s, when it seemed possible that enough states would petition for a convention to consider a balanced budget amendment. Between 1973 and 1992, 22 bills and resolutions to enact congressional procedures that would be implemented in response to a successful call for an Article V Convention were introduced in the House of Representatives, while 17 were introduced in the Senate. Generally styled the "Constitutional Convention Procedures Act," or some similar title, these bills were the subject of extensive hearings in both houses. They sought to provide by law for standards and procedures which Congress would follow in the event two-thirds of the states called for an Article V Convention.[63] The content of these proposals is examined at greater length in the companion to this report, CRS Report R42589, *The Article V Convention to Propose Constitutional Amendments: Contemporary Issues for Congress*.

The Role of the States in an Article V Convention

An Article V Convention for proposing amendments to the Constitution can only be called when the legislatures of two-thirds of the states submit applications. Beyond its simple mandate, the Constitution is mute on the details of enabling procedure, which would necessarily involve a broad range of actions within the legislatures, while also posing significant questions of procedure in the states.

Proposing a Convention: Actions in the State Legislatures

The legislatures of the several states are fundamental to a potential Article V Convention. The applications or petitions to Congress must come from these bodies. The Constitution, however, provides minimal guidance for the state petition process, stating only the end result, that Congress should call a convention on "... the Application of the Legislatures of two thirds of the several

---

[62] According to the FOAVC website, between 1988 and 2010, Alabama, Arizona, Florida, Georgia, Idaho, Louisiana, Montana, New Hampshire, Nevada, North Dakota, Oklahoma, Oregon, South Carolina, South Dakota, Tennessee, Utah and Wyoming rescinded Article V applications. See FOAVC website, at http://foavc.org/file.php/1/Amendments. In recent years, however, Alabama, Florida, and New Hampshire have submitted new applications for a convention to consider a balanced budget amendment. The author gratefully credits Gregory Watson, Legislative Assistant with the Texas Legislature for assistance in verifying this list.

[63] These proposals are examined in greater detail in the companion to this report, CRS Report R42589, *The Article V Convention to Propose Constitutional Amendments: Contemporary Issues for Congress*, by Thomas H. Neale.

States." With well over a century of experience in proposing an Article V Convention, the states have arrived at certain precedents for the consideration of these applications.

Action by Both Houses Required

First, it may be inferred that the founders intended that applications come from both houses of state legislatures: bicameralism was the prevailing practice at the time of the Philadelphia Convention, although several states retained the single-house legislatures established by their early revolutionary constitutions.[64] Available documentation tends to support the conclusion that Article V Convention applications must be approved in both chambers of the proposing legislature. The single modern exception is Nebraska, whose legislature is unicameral.

Choice of Legislative Vehicle

Proceeding from bicameral approval, the states in the past four decades have employed a range of parliamentary instruments drawn from their diverse political experience as vehicles for an Article V Convention application. These include concurrent resolutions (most common), joint resolutions, single-chamber resolutions passed by both houses of the legislature, concurrent memorials, and single-chamber memorials passed by both houses.

Legislative Procedure

Moving beyond the general agreement that a state application, in order to be valid, must be approved by the joint or concurrent action of *both* of its legislative chambers, further questions have been raised concerning the standards that would apply. These include

- What margin is necessary for an application to be valid? Would a plurality vote be sufficient, or would a simple majority, or super majority be required?

- Beyond margin requirements, would approval of an application petition require a majority of the whole membership, or approval by members present and voting?

- Could the upper and lower chambers of the same state legislature adopt different quorum or vote margin standards?

The historical record provides some guidance: a 1981 Congressional Research Service report for Congress found that states tended to require that their legislatures approve applications for an Article V Convention by the same supermajorities they impose for proposals to amend their own constitutions.[65] Currently, 33 states provide that constitutional amendments be approved by a supermajority of both legislative chambers, with requirements ranging from three-fifths (60%) to three-fourths (75%) of the whole membership in both houses.[66] This question was addressed in most of the constitutional convention procedures bills introduced in Congress in the 1980s and

---

[64] Three states established unicameral legislatures in their original constitutions. Georgia and Pennsylvania moved to bicameralism in 1789 and 1790, respectively, while Vermont continued with a single-chamber state legislature until 1836. Source: National Council of State Legislatures at http://www.ncsl.org/?tabid=13544.

[65] Congressional Research Service Report to Congress 81-135 GOV/A, *Constitutional Conventions: Political and Legal Issues, the Unanswered Questions*, by Meredith McCoy and David C. Huckabee (Washington: CRS, 1981), p. 10. Available to congressional staff from the author of this report.

[66] Council of State Governments, *The Book of the States*, 2010 edition, volume 42 (Lexington, KY: 2010), p. 13.

1990s. Most earlier bills provided that "... the State legislature shall follow the rules of procedure that govern the enactment of a statute [that is, a normal state law]...."[67] Later bills tended to differ, leaving the states to determine such requirements, e.g., "... the rules of procedure governing the adoption or withdrawal of a resolution ... are determinable by the State legislature...."[68]

Should the states extend any of their existing standards to applications for an Article V Convention? It may be argued that establishing clearly defined procedures and standards before considering a convention application might answer legal and constitutional uncertainties and reduce the likelihood of a successful challenge to the validity of an application.

State Applications for an Article V Convention: Scope and Conditions

Here again, the Constitution offers little guidance on the petition process for an Article V Convention. A range of questions concerning the content of petitions remains to be answered. What is the permissible scope of state applications? May they call for a general convention, or must they be confined to a single issue? If they do address a single issue, must they be identical, or is general similarity sufficient? To which persons or what offices must the states address applications? For how long do applications remain valid? May a state legislature vote to rescind an Article V application?

Must Applications Share Identical Language or Is Issue Congruency Sufficient?

With some notable exceptions, most commentators hold that state applications for a convention must address the same issue in order to be counted toward the two-thirds threshold established by the Constitution, but they need not be identical.

First, and most obviously, there is no *constitutional* mandate that the petitions be identical, although the Constitution seldom descends to such level of detail. The House Judiciary Committee, in a 1993 study, concluded that "[t]he applications need not be exact copies of each other. On the contrary, most commentators suggest that Congress should be generous in its interpretation.... Applying too strict a standard could be viewed as an attempt to prevent the States from exercising their option under Article V."[69] The American Bar Association's Constitutional Convention Study Committee expressed a similar view in its 1974 report, noting that, "[w]e agree with the suggestion that it should not be necessary that each application be identical or propose similar changes in the same subject matter."[70]

As one witness at the Senate Judiciary Subcommittee on the Constitution's 1979 hearings noted, "Article V seems to require a general consensus among two-thirds of the States that a

---

[67] S. 1272, 93rd Cong., 2nd sess., "Federal Constitutional Procedures Act," Section 3(a).

[68] S. 214, 102nd Cong., 1st sess., "Constitutional Convention Implementation Act of 1991," Section 3(a).

[69] U.S. Congress, House, Committee on the Judiciary, *Is There a Constitutional Convention in Our Future?* 103rd Cong., 1st sess., committee print, serial no. 1(Washington: GPO, 1993) p. 7.

[70] American Bar Association, Special Constitutional Convention Study Subcommittee, *Amendment of the Constitution by the Convention Method Under Article V* (Chicago?: American Bar Association, 1974), p. 31.

Constitutional Convention be called. Thus, only those applications which request a Convention to deal with the same issue should be counted."[71] Legislative language in earlier proposed constitutional convention procedures bills supported this interpretation, without requiring that they be identical. For instance, S. 214, introduced by Senator Orrin Hatch in the 102nd Congress stated that applications, in order to be valid, must call for "a constitutional convention on the same subject matter ...."[72] Similarly, S. 1272, introduced in the 93rd Congress by Senator Sam Ervin, proposed that valid applications "stat[e] the nature of the amendment or amendments to be proposed."[73] The Friends of an Article V Convention, FOAVC, perhaps the leading proponent of an Article V Convention, claims that such questions are immaterial, maintaining that one petition is as good as another. FOAVC asserts that as soon as Congress received applications from two-thirds of the states for a convention on any subject, or for a general convention, it was under obligation to call a convention. The framers, they maintain, deliberately avoided a specific requirement that applications be identical or similar. By FOAVC's reckoning, 49 of the 50 states[74] have, at some time or another, submitted an Article V petition, and Congress was obligated to call a convention not later than 1911.[75]

Conditional Applications

Beyond the question of similarity, some constitutional commentators have expressed concern over state applications encumbered by various conditions. For instance, during the balanced budget amendment convention drive of the 1980s, a number of state instruments declared their applications would be null and void if Congress proposed a balanced budget amendment. Others asserted their applications would be valid only if a convention were limited to the specific issue in question.[76] Writing during the same period of the various state applications then in hand, one observer noted that "[e]ven if the intent is clear, the existing applications represent a 'hodge podge' of proposals, and at least 16 petitions call for a convention only in the face of congressional inaction on the subject. Whether such conditional requests remain valid is unknown...."[77]

Another class of problematic applications in the 1980s were those that proposed specific amendment language. Some would have accepted a "substantially similar" amendment, while others attempted to limit the convention solely to consideration of their particular amendments. In its 1993 study, the House Judiciary Committee indicated the former might be qualified, but that

> ... an application requesting an up-or-down vote on a specifically worded amendment cannot be considered valid. Such an approach robs the Convention of its deliberative function which

---

[71] Testimony of Douglas Voegeler, in: U.S. Congress, Senate , *Constitutional Convention Procedures: Hearings on S. 3, S. 520, and S. 1710 Before the Subcommittee on the Constitution of the Senate Committee on the Judiciary*, 96th Cong., 1st sess. (Washington, 1980: GPO), p. 769.

[72] S. 214, 102nd Cong., "Constitutional Convention Implementation Act of 1991," Section 6a.

[73] S. 1272, 93rd Cong., "Federal Constitutional Convention Procedures Act," Section 2.

[74] Gregory Watson, Legislative Assistant with the Texas State Legislature identified Hawaii as the single exception. E-mail exchange, July 30, 2012.

[75] Friends of an Article V Convention, FOAVC, Article V Application Tables, available at http://www.foa5c.org/file.php/1/Articles/Table_Summarizing_State_Applications.pdf.

[76] *Is There a Constitutional Convention in America's Future?* Committee Print, p. 6.

[77] Meredith McCoy, "Balanced Budget Amendment: Congress Versus the States?" *Federal Bar News*, volume 26, no. 4, April 1979 p. 101.

---

is inherent in [A]rticle V language stating that the Convention's purpose is to "propose amendments." If the State legislatures were permitted to propose the exact wording of an amendment and stipulate that the language not be altered, the Convention would be deprived of this function and would become instead part of the ratification process.[78]

Former Solicitor General Walter Dellinger has further argued that exact language proposals "short-circuit" the checks and balances built into Article V by the founders. They intended, he asserts, to provide sub-federal communities, embodied in the states, the authority to propose a convention to consider amendments, but deliberately refrained from giving the state legislatures the power to determine the exact text of the amendments to be proposed.[79]

The proposal to authorize the states to propose specifically worded amendments in their applications for an Article V Convention is generally referred to as the Madison Amendment, for the fourth President, who favored it during his career in the House of Representatives. A version of the Madison Amendment, H.J.Res. 57, has been introduced in the 112th Congress, and is discussed in the companion to this report, CRS Report R42589, *The Article V Convention to Propose Constitutional Amendments: Contemporary Issues for Congress.*

Timeliness/Contemporaneity

Another question concerning state Article V Convention applications is their timeliness or contemporaneity—for what period should an application be considered valid?

The advocacy group Friends of an Article V Convention (FOAVC) asserts that there is no set time limit on the validity of state applications, and that Congress has no authority to set one. They claim that since the Constitution offers no guidance on this question, state applications remain valid indefinitely. As a related example, they point to the 27th Amendment, which was pending before the states from 1789 to 1992, until it was ultimately ratified.[80]

Conversely, the House Judiciary Committee reported in 1993 that there was "general agreement" that state applications for an Article V Convention should not remain valid indefinitely. The report cited seven years, the now-traditional qualifying period for proposed constitutional amendments, as a time limit widely favored by constitutional scholars.[81] It should be noted that this is also the period proposed in most congressional constitutional convention procedures bills. Other commentators have suggested a two- or four-year "shelf life" for state applications, as this would presumably give state legislatures that meet biennially the opportunity to submit an application.[82] Moreover, in justification of the shorter period, the Judiciary Committee noted that the application process "is a matter of lesser finality than an amendment to the Constitution for all time."[83]

---

[78] *Is There a Constitutional Convention in America's Future?* p. 6.

[79] Walter E. Dellinger, "The Recurring Question of the 'Limited' Constitutional Convention," *Yale Law Journal*, volume 88, issue 8, July 1979, p. 1632.

[80] FOAVC Frequently Asked Questions Page, "What Does Contemporaneous Mean as it Relates to Counting Applications," available at http://foavc.org/file.php/1/Articles/FAQ.htm#Contemporaneous.

[81] *Is There A Constitutional Convention in America's Future?* p. 10.

[82] "Proposed Legislation on the Convention Method of Amending the United States Constitution," Note, *Harvard Law Review*, volume 85, issue 8, June 1972, pp. 1619-1621.

[83] *Is There A Constitutional Convention in America's Future?* p. 10.

May a State Amend or Rescind Its Application for an Article V Convention?

During the 1970s and 1980s, 32 states submitted applications for a convention to consider an amendment to require a balanced federal budget except in extraordinary circumstances. As noted earlier in this report, support for a convention faltered in some states, while supporters of 1985's Gramm-Rudman-Hollings Balanced Budget and Emergency Deficit Control Act (GRH)[84] claimed the legislation would serve the same purpose as an Article V Convention with less risk.[85] As interest in a convention waned, and concern grew over the prospect of a runaway convention, a number of states reconsidered their applications for a convention. As also noted, between 1988 and 2010, 17 state legislatures had passed resolutions of rescission. In some cases, these resolutions rescinded *all* previous Article V applications, while others also specifically cited a convention for a balanced budget amendment.[86]

Here again, a decision on the status of these rescissions has never been made, largely because the 34-state requirement has never been met. As with so many other aspects of the Article V Convention issue, opinion is divided. Some constitutional scholars hold that the application process is only preliminary, and that states may withdraw their applications without prejudice, so long as the two-thirds threshold has not been crossed.[87] Others assert that an application carries the same weight as a state's ratification of a constitutional amendment, which cannot be rescinded. Many of the constitutional convention procedures bills introduced in Congress from the 1970s through the 1990s authorized states to rescind their applications, so long as the constitutional threshold had not been met. It should be noted, however, that in the past, Congress refused to accept rescissions of state ratifications of the 14th Amendment, apparently reflecting the viewpoint cited above. These refusals were ultimately upheld by the Supreme Court, which determined in *Coleman v. Miller* that rescission fell under the "political question" rule, and that Congress, therefore, possessed "the ultimate authority" to set rules for "the promulgation of the adoption of the amendment."[88]

May a State Application Contain a Self-Canceling Provision?

In the past, a number of applications for an Article V Convention have also included self-canceling clauses which stated that the application would be null and void in the event Congress proposed an amendment that achieved the same effect as that called for in the application. This practice is associated with "prodding," as identified earlier in this report. According to the House Judiciary Committee's 1993 report, this strategy "does not necessarily render an application invalid.... However, applications containing different conditions may not necessarily be counted together to determine whether a Convention must be called."[89]

---

[84] 99 Stat. 1038.

[85] Caplan, *Constitutional Brinksmanship*, pp. 83-85.

[86] See above under "Balanced Budget Amendment" for FOAVC's list of state rescissions.

[87] Dwight Connely, "Amending the Constitution: Is This Any Way to Call for a Constitutional Convention?" *Arizona Law Review*, volume 22, issue 4, 1980, pp.1033-1034.

[88] *Coleman v. Miller*, 307 U.S. 433 (1939) at 450. The political question doctrine refers to policy issues in which the courts, or specifically the Supreme Court, have declined to decide, on the grounds that political questions are properly resolved in the political process, not by judicial ruling.

[89] *Is There a Constitutional Convention in America's Future?*, p. 6.

Submitting the Applications to Congress

The final action by a state legislature that has approved an application for an Article V Convention is to transmit news of its action to the appropriate authorities. The Constitution offers no advice on this question, and in fact, the House Judiciary Committee's 1993 report noted that states had sent applications for a balanced budget convention to a wide range of congressional officials, including the Clerk of the House, the Secretary of the Senate, the Speaker of the House, the President of the Senate, the President pro tempore of the Senate, both sets of congressional officials, other officials, the Library of Congress, and "to no one in particular." According to the report, there were even instances in which applications were *not* forwarded by the states.[90] For the record, many of the state petitions printed in the *Congressional Record* that were reviewed by the author of this report specifically noted that copies would also be delivered to the Senators and Representatives of the state's congressional delegation.

So, the final decisions are currently made by the officers of the state legislatures themselves. Congress could establish regular procedures for transmission, recordation, and retention of state applications, and an argument can be made that more information is better in this instance. The Speaker and Clerk of the House, the Vice President, President Pro-Tempore, Secretary of the Senate, and the Archivist of the United States would be perhaps the most obvious candidates to be recipients of Article V Convention applications. In addition, notification of a state's Senators and Representatives, as has been done in some earlier instances, might also be considered a courtesy, particularly in light of the fact that members of the state's congressional delegation could serve as well-placed advocates for the Article V Convention.

A Role for the State Governor?

Do the state governors have any responsibilities in the Article V state petition process? The balance of opinion on this question is that they do not. The House Judiciary Committee's 1993 study states that "[w]hen article V specifies that a Convention be called 'upon the applications of the *legislatures*,' that is exactly what it means (emphasis added)."[91] The Supreme Court's 1798 decision in *Hollingsworth v. Virginia*, which held that the President's approval is not required for a constitutional amendment proposed by Congress, is cited in support of this argument.[92] One legal scholar asserted that, by extension, "[s]ince the President is excluded at the national level, the reasonable conclusion is that the State Governors should also be excluded."[93] A 1974 American Bar Association report appears to confirm this view, noting that, "the results of a questionnaire-type survey ... indicate that a substantial majority [of states] exclude the governor from participation...."[94]

Some commentators have differed from these prevailing views. In his 1972 letter to then-House Judiciary Committee Chairman Emmanuel Celler, constitutional scholar Charles Black asserted that

---

[90] Ibid., p. 12.

[91] *Is There a Constitutional Convention in Our Future?*, p. 11.

[92] 3 U.S. (3 Dall.) 378 (1798). The Court ruled that the President's signature on a proposed amendment was permissible, but carried no constitutional force.

[93] Connely, "Amending the Constitution: Is This Any Way to Call for a Constitutional Convention?," p.1030.

[94] American Bar Association, *Amendment of the Constitution by the Convention Method Under Article V*, p. 45.

... the amendment process should not be made easy, and the inclusion in it of the governors of the states, popularly elected statewide, would be a desirable further check.... What possible reason can there be for ordaining that so solemn a step as a State's applying for a national constitutional convention is to go through an *easier* process than a state law changing the speed limit? (emphasis in the original)[95]

Another observer concurred during the 1979 hearings before the Senate Judiciary Committee's Subcommittee on the Constitution, asserting that state governors could be included in the process. While not suggesting that Congress attempt to require participation by the governors, he urged that they not be excluded, because in his opinion, they are best able to reflect the views of the broadest range of citizens within their states. This writer went on to note that governors are elected by citizens on a statewide basis and suggested that they would be less likely to be subject to distortions of the public interest that might be caused by gerrymandering in the legislatures.[96]

Finally, the record reveals considerable variation in state practices. The House Judiciary Subcommittee on Civil and Constitutional Rights noted in 1993 that governors were not completely excluded from the process. A survey of state legislatures' petitions in the balanced budget amendment campaign in the 1970s and 1980s revealed that 9 of 32 applications had been referred to state governors for approval. Of these, seven were "signed or otherwise approved by the governor," one was returned to the legislature unsigned with the governor's explanation that his signature was unnecessary, and in the last case, the governor took no action and offered no explanation.[97]

Concluding Observations

The Article V Convention for proposing amendments was the subject of considerable debate and forethought at the Constitutional Convention. The founders clearly intended it as a balance to proposal of amendments by Congress, providing the people, through their state legislatures, with an alternative means to consider amendments, particularly if Congress was unable or unwilling to act on its own. Since it is one of the few provisions of the Constitution that has never been implemented, however, the Article V Convention presents many questions for Congress. This report has provided relevant historical and external perspectives, intended to assist Members and their staff in consideration of this issue. A companion report, CRS Report R42589, *The Article V Convention to Propose Constitutional Amendments: Contemporary Issues for Congress*, provides a complementary exposition and analysis of the potential role of Congress in the process. In the event a convention became a serious possibility, Members and staff could also draw on a large body of scholarly writing on the subject, and not least, the work and products of two decades of serious congressional consideration of the Article V Convention process from the 1970s to the 1990s.

---

[95] Charles Black, "Amending the Constitution: A Letter to a Congressman," *Yale Law Journal*, volume 82, number 2, December 1972, p. 210.

[96] Testimony of Kenneth Kofmehl, in U.S. Congress, Senate, *Constitutional Convention Procedures: Hearings on S. 3, S. 520, and S. 1710 Before the Subcommittee on the Constitution of the Senate Committee on the Judiciary*, 96th Congress, 1st sess. (Washington, 1980: GPO), p. 447.

[97] *Is There a Constitutional Convention in Our Future?*, p. 11.

Author Contact Information

Thomas H. Neale
Specialist in American National Government
tneale@crs.loc.gov, 7-7883